Notes to my Daughter

A FATHER'S BLITZ DIARY

ALEXANDER PIERCE

EDITED BY CHRISTINE CUSS

All royalties due to the author shall be donated to the Royal British Legion for the support of wounded troops returning from Afghanistan, and also to the wives and families of those who sadly lost their lives. Many will need support well into their old age.

Front: (foreground) Christine one week after the bombing; (background) Christine's tenth birthday party. *Back:* Alexander, Gwendoline and Christine Pierce. Poppy logo © Royal British Legion. All effort has been taken to trace images used to original source.

First published 2010

The History Press
The Mill, Brimscombe Port
Stroud, Gloucestershire, GL5 2QG
www.thehistorypress.co.uk

British Library Cataloguing in Publication Data.
A catalogue record for this book is available from the British Library.

ISBN 978 0 7524 5554 9

Typesetting and origination by The History Press
Printed in Great Britain
Manufacturing managed by Jellyfish Print Solutions Ltd

Contents

Foreword

The capturing of memories for future generations is always a very great service. Christine Cuss, in providing a wider readership with the diary written for her by her father, Alexander, allows the reader to enter her world and that of so many other children who lived through the years leading up and encompassing the devastation of the Second World War.

Christine Cuss has presented the text of her father's diary very faithfully indeed and the straightforward and often brief entries serve only to give a greater clarity to events that were so important for a father thinking of his only child. A document such as this forms an important contribution to our understanding of everyday life of a difficult and deeply significant period in our nation's history.

At a time when the world once more faces many uncertainties, and families are called upon to carry the burden of separation brought about through the demands placed upon our armed services, the words of this diary will find a fresh resonance for many. May it also bring a sense of hope through the commitment to family life that is so evident in the pages of this book.

Richard Moth
Bishop of the Forces

A Father's Diary

My father, Alexander Pierce, was born in Mortlake, Surrey in 1904, and was one of eight children. His eldest brother Bill was killed in the First World War. Because of this, my father left school early and joined the army, misleading them about his age. His education, therefore, was poor, so readers of his diary will observe many spelling mistakes, but that is what makes the diary so special, because it was written by a very ordinary man whose thoughts and fears represented so many during those terrible war years.

My father married Gwendoline and they lived in her parents' house in Hammersmith, West London. I was born on 17 July 1934, and that was the day my father began his diary to me. His intention was to record various events in my life, like my first tooth etc. Little did he know that within a short while his entries would one day become a historic document.

Although I was an only child I had many friends and there were always uncles and aunts popping in. My mother supplemented the family income by making beautiful blouses at home for a West End company, often working well into the evening whilst dad kept me amused, before the war began. Sometimes I sat by my mother at her sewing machine and she taught me how to sew neatly, often making me unpick something if it was not right. We were a very happy family who enjoyed days at the seaside and

17. July. 1934

Christine Born at 4.15 P.M.

Tuesday 22. Jan. 1935
Christine posed for Artist
Model it was acepted and hung
@ the Royal. Acddamey
called. Madona of. the Bay

September 1934
    Mother goes in to Hospital

June 1935
    Christine cuts her. first two
teeth she was eleven months
old.

holidays spent in my grandparents' second home at Herne Bay for the first five years of my life, prior to the advent of war. However, when war came, it brought so many changes.

One of the most difficult decisions my parents had to make was whether to send me away for evacuation or not. Readers will be touched by the entry my father made on 1 December 1939: anguish felt by so many parents.

My father's aim in life was to do his best to look after my mother and me, and he was very determined that I should receive the education that he lacked. I well remember him setting me a page of sums to do every day which I completed before he came home from work. So often my lessons were done in air-raid shelters, and every evening we went to sleep in a public air-raid shelter joined by all the neighbours. Had we not done this, we would not have survived the destruction of my home by a doodlebug in 1944.

Looking back on the time between 1943 and 1945, life must have been intolerable for my parents and grandmother as they had so much tragedy and sadness with which to cope.

I sat the eleven-plus examination as the war ended and my parents were so proud when I passed the entrance examination to go to the Godolphin and Latymer School in West London, one of London's top schools. I settled well into my new life at a school that not only gave me a wonderful education, but which also broadened my horizons. We had survived the war and my parents had realised their ambition for their daughter.

Christine Cuss *née* Pierce

1934

17 July 1934

Christine Born at 4.15 P.M.

—

September 1934

Mother goes in to Hospital.

—

1935

22 January 1935

Christine posed for Artist model it was acepted and hung @ the Royal. Acadamey called Madona of the Bay.

—

June 1935

Christine cuts her first two teeth, she was eleven months old.

—

20 July 1935

Mother goes in to Hospital for operation appendix.

—

1 September 1935

Went to Herne Bay for our Holidays, very nice time.

—

1936

20 January 1936

King George V died @ 11.55 P.M.

—

28 January 1936

Mother and myself went to see the funeral procession got up @ 5.30 A.M.

—

30 January 1936

Grandad Morris went in to Hospital, operation for his Eyes.

—

22 February 1936

Put 8.13.0. in the Bank for Christine. I hope she will kiss her Daddy some day for it.

—

10 March 1936

Christine went to the pictures for the first time.

Wednesday June 10th 1936
Christine had to go to hospital
with a bad eye.

Sat 4th July 1936
Christine went to Caister
nr. Great Yarmouth for our
holidays. We did not like it
rained for 3 days.

Thursday July 16. 1936
An attempt on the Kings
Life a man was arrested
and charged @ Bow St. Station

17 July 1936
Christine Birthday
2 years old.

War between Italy and Abyssinian. Abyssinian were defeated.

10 May 1936

Christine and Mother went to Jaywick Sands, very nice time.

—

1 June 1936

Christine went to the Zoo Rengents Park.

—

10 June 1936

Christine had to go to hospital with a bad eye.

—

4 July 1936

Christine went to Caister Nr Great Yarmouth for our holidays. We did not like it. Rained for 3 days.

—

16 July 1936

An attempt on the Kings life, a man was arrested and charged @ Bow St Station.

—

Wed 2nd Sept 1936
Christine went to Brighton
for the Day

Frid 11. Sept 1936
This is the First stamp
of King Edwards Reign

Wed. Nov. 11. 1936
Christine Went to Herne Bay
for the day very Wet

Thursday 3rd Dec 1936
King Edward causes a Sensation
he wants to Marry a Mrs Simpson
who as been married twice and
divorce twice. The Country is very
up set we are waiting to here what
is going to be done

17 July 1936

Christine Birthday.
2 years old.

—

26 July 1936

King Edward unveiled War Memorial to the Canadians
who fell @ Vimy Ridge.

—

3 August 1936

Took Christine to see Buckingham Palace and the
changing of the Guards.

—

16 August 1936

We took Christine to Brighton and had a good day.
Christine messed on my trousers.

—

28 August 1936

Christine went to Hampton Court with Mother.

—

"SOME TIME BEFORE I RETURN"

In his farewell broadcast Edward VIII, speaking of his departure from England, said:

"It may be some time before I return to my native land, but I shall always follow the fortunes of the British race and Empire with profound interest, and if at any time in the future I can be found of service to His Majesty in a private station I shall not fail. . . . God bless you all. God save the King."

Final quote from Edward VIII's broadcast before leaving the country.

2 September 1936

Christine went to Brighton for the Day.

—

11 September 1936

This is the first stamp of King Edward's Reign.

—

11 November 1936

Christine went to Herne Bay for the day, very wet.

—

3 December 1936

King Edward causes a sensation he wants to marry a Mrs Simpson who as been married twice and divorce twice. The Crountry is very up set we are waiting to here what is going to bc donc.

—

10 December 1936

King Edward the Eighth renounces the Throne.

—

Duke of York to be made King.

—

11 December 1936

King Edward spoke to his people for the last time over the Wireless.

—

12 December 1936

Duke of York proclaimed King of England.

—

31 December 1936

Christine asleep while Mother and myself went to church to see the old year out and the new one in.
The end of 1936.

—

1937

January 1937

Christine has got a doll and she calls it Faggy it is ever so dirty and she loves it more than all the others.

—

27 January 1937

Christine had a touch of flue been in bed for 2 days, much better now.

—

1 February 1937

Christine very ill pains in her Tum Tum and back and her Eyes. Took her to the Doctors and he said it was her liver, much better now.

—

7 February 1937

Went to Fred's and Mary's with Christine and Christine took Faggy. When we came home we left Faggy there we feel up set about it but Christine has taken to her other one.

Wed 24. March. 1937
Christine saw the Boat Race
Oxford Won by 3 lengths
after losing for 13 consecutive
   years

Fried 26. March. 1937
Christine Mother and Myself
went to Herne Bay for 3 days
had a good time but very cold

May 12. 1937
Coronation of King George VI
Christine went to a tea party

May 24. 1937
Went to Herne Bay with
Christine she had a good
time fine weather

24 March 1937

Christine cut her last two teeth @ 2 years and 8 months old.

—

Christine saw the Boat Race. Oxford Won by 3 lengths after losing for 13 consecutive years.

—

26 March 1937

Christine Mother and Myself went to Herne Bay for 3 days, had a good time but very cold.

—

12 May 1937

Coronation of King George VI. Christine went to a tea party.

—

24 May 1937

Went to Herne Bay with Christine, she had a good time, fine weather.

—

3 June 1937

The Duke of Windsor got married to Mrs Simpson in France. No Royal Family attended.

—

14 June 1937

Christine went to Southend for the day with Mother, had a good time.

—

16 June 1937

Christine went to Ascot Races in Uncle Tom's car. Told me all about the horses, said she sat on Tom's shoulders.

—

4 July 1937

Christine went to Weymouth with us for our holidays, we had a good time. The landlady said that Christine was the Best child she'd had there. We went to:
Porltand Bill
Upwey Wishing Wells
Bowleaye Cove
Sandsfoot Castle

—

13 July 1937

Christine gone with Mother to Herne Bay for 3 days.

—

17 July 1937

Christine's Birthday. She had a party, she had 4 children and 4 adults and 16 birthday cards. Late night.

—

2 August 1937

Went for a ride in Tom's car with Christine. Christine saw:
Windsor Great Park
Windsor Castle
and stoped @ Walton on Thames and had tea with Dorothy's Mother. Very enjoyable ride out.

—

21 August 1937

Christine saw Aunt Lizzie for the first time, she came up with Percy for week end.

—

22 August 1937

Christine went with us to Littlehampton in Tom's car, we had a very good day indeed. Coming back we called @ Worthing. Christine enjoyed it very much.

—

15 September 1937

Christine went to see the State Apartments @ Windsor Castle with Cyril and Mother.

—

25 September 1937

Christine went with us to Herne Bay for a week. She went and saw Canterbury Cathedral.

—

18 October 1937

Christine saw Queen Mary out side West London Hospital.

—

26 November 1937

We brought a new Dolly for Christine. The other one was so dirty we had to get rid of it, Lucy was its name. I don't thinks she likes it so much as the old one.

Alexander, Gwendoline and Christine Pierce aged 2 years.

27 November 1937

We took Christine out round the shops to see the toys. She does not like Father Christmas so I took her to get use't to seeing him. We saw him in one of the stores, I got her to shake hands with him, she told him she wanted a dolly's Pram and a new Doll. She fills quite bucked now.

—

11 December 1937

Christine had a boil on her leg very bad, to her way of thinking but we soon got it better.

—

31 December 1937

Christine, this is the end of 1937 we have had a very good year, Mother and myself went to church to see the old year out and new year in.

—

1938

1 January 1938

Christine, we took you to see your first Pantomime, it was called Cinderella, you enjoyed it very much.

—

8 January 1938

Christine saw her second Pantomime called Jack and Jill @ King's Theatre. She had the tooth ache.

—

10 January 1938

Mother took Christine to Tite St. Hospital to have her teeth out, she has got to go again on tuesday, she has got a swollen face.

—

11 January 1938

Christine had 3 teeth out, Mother said she was a good girl, she never cryed @ all. She was 3½ years old.

—

Monday 14 March 1938

Christine I am writing this page for you, to let you see the state of the World @ this present time First Mossolini Invaded and took Abyssinian. now Hitler of Germany has invaded Austria. These to Dictators are causing all the trouble that is going on. All I hope is that Germany will not interfere with cyecho-Slovakian because England has made a promiss to go to her assistance, that would mean we would have to go to War which I do not want because I should have to leave you and Mother

I love you both

18 January 1938

Christine in bed with the measles, Doctor Mason came to see her, she is 3½ years old.

—

14 March 1938

Christine, I am writing this page for you, to let you see the state of the World @ this presant time. First Mossolini [Mussolini] invaded and took Abyssinian. Now Hitler of Germany has invaded Austria. These to Dictators are causing all the trouble that is going on. All I hope is that Germany will not interfere with Czecho-Slovakian because England has made a promise to go to her assistance, that would mean we would have to go to war which I do not want because I should have to leave you and Mother.

<u>I Love you both.</u>

—

25 June 1938

Christine, we took you with us to Herne Bay for our holidays, we had a good time. You went with us to Canterbury Cathedral, Reculver and saw the Ruins.

—

12 Sept 1938

Dear Christine

we are now passing through a
most critical time. It looks as if
Germany is going to invade,
Czecho-Slovakia, that would
mean another World War which
I spoke of further back in this
book. The Prime Minister of England
Neville Chamberlain has sent for
the Prime Minster of France to come
to England. You have been up
to Downing St to day which is
the 18th of Sept while the cabinet
is sitting we are waiting to here
what the news is going to be
We all hope it is not War
            Love Daddy .

16 July 1938

We had a birthday party for Christine, she had 5 little children. We had a very nice time indeed, Christine had 11 birthday cards and lots of presants.

—

17 July 1938

Christine Birthday, we took her for the day to Clacton on Sea. We had a very good day out indeed, there was 9 adults. We all had tea @ Butlins Holiday Camp.

—

24 July 1938

Christine went with us to Walton on Thames. To Dorothy's Mother's, we had tea there and went out in a boat for a ride. We did not enjoy ourselfs very much.

—

13 August 1938

Christine went to Herne Bay with Mother for the week, had a good time.

—

24 August 1938

Christine can count up to Eleven quite easy, she is 4 years old.

—

12 September 1938

Dear Christine
We are now passing through a most critical time. It looks as if Germany is going to invade, Czecho-Slovakia, that would mean another World War which I spoke of further back in this book. The Prime Minister of England Neville Chamberlain has sent for the Prime Minister of France to come to England. You have been up to Downing St to day which is the 18th of Sept, while the cabinet is sitting we are waiting to here what the news is going to be. We all hope it is not War.
Love Daddy.

—

18 September 1938

Dear Christine
We have taken you this day to Westminster Abbey for the church service, there were thousands of people there, you went to sleep after a while, you had a nasty cold but we hope it will soon get better.
Love Daddy.

—

Sunday 25 Sept 1938

We all went to get fitted with
gas maskes christine you cryed
a lot, it upset mothers a lot
but it had to be done, to
save your life in case war
was declaired ~~witch~~ which is
supposed to be Oct 1st.

Thursday 29th Sept
Mother went to get our gas
masks she got ~~my~~ mine and herrs
but she was told she would
have to go to the Town Hall
for christines it has up set mother
because she thinks they will
take you from her to sent you
away for safety

Thursday 29ᵉʳᵈ Sept 1938

At this time of writing things are very bad indeed war is supposed to be declared on Oct 1ˢᵗ 1938 but @ the last moment Hitler of Germany sent for M'. Chamberlain the Premier of England to have a last talk to see if they can bring about a peacefull solution this in my opinion about it, is that Hitler as got the wind up.

———   ———

Frid 30 Sept 1938

at the time of writing this note there is great rejoicing all over the World, because the four Great Powers namely :-

25 September 1938

We all went to get fitted with gas masks, Christine you cried a lot, it upset Mother a lot but it had to be done, to save your life in case war was declaired which is supposed to be Oct 1st.

—

29 September 1938

Mother went to get our gas masks, she got mine and hers but she was told she would have to go to the Town Hall for Christines, it has upset Mother because she thinks they will take you from her to sent you away for safety.
At this time of writing things are very bad indeed, war is supposed to be declared on Oct 1st 1938 but @ the last moment Hitler of Germany sent for Mr Chamberlain the Premier of England to have a last talk to see if they can bring about a peaceful solution, this is my opinion about it, is that Hitler as got the wind up.

—

30 September 1938

At the time of writing this note there is great rejoicing all over the World, because the four Great Powers namely Italy, Germany, France, Gt. Britain have come to an agreement over the Czech problem so @ the last minute war has been adverted.

Dec 19th 1938 Monday
    Christine wrote her name
by her self @ 4½ years of age
                copied from me

CHRISTINE
PIERCE

13 November 1938

Christine went to Joanie's Birthday party, she had a very good time.

—

16 November 1938

This is a dawring [drawing] done by Christine @ the age of 4 years.

—

4 December 1938

Christine went to see cousin Barbara's Christening.

—

Barbara was born Nov 3rd 1938.

—

19 December 1938

Christine wrote her name by her self @ 4½ years of age, copied from me.

—

24 December 1938

Christine very bad cold had to put her to bed, she was very bad all over Christmas, she is much better now.

31 December 1938

Last day of the year, Mother and myself went to church to see the old year out and new one in. This has been a very good year for us, we hope 1939 will be as good.

Love Mother and Dad
PS Mother is working very hard making Blouses, she is very good to you. I love you both.

—

1939

24 January 1939

Christine was to have started school, but she was ever so sick Monday night that we kept her @ home.

—

25 January 1939

Christine started school, it was snowing very hard, Christine said she loved it, she is 4½ years old, her first school friend was Kathleen Mills.

—

15 March 1939

Dear Christine
I had made this entry in this book to let you see how things are going on in the World. Hitler of Germany has broken the agreement with this Crountry and he as marched into Czecho-Slovakia, This man is causing a lot of trouble but he will get what he is asking for before long.
Love Dad.

—

Wednesday 15 March 1939

Dear Christine.
I had made this entry in this
book to let you see how things are
going on in the World. Hitler of
Germany has broken the agreement
with this brountry and he as marchai
into Czecho-Slovakia, This man is
causing a lot of trouble but he
will get what he is asking for
before long . Love Dad .

_____

Monday 20 March 1939
Christine has got a touch of Flue
Mother has kept her away from
school for this week I hope she
will be better soon. love Dad

Tuesday March 28th 1939
Christine examined by the Doctor
@ the school he said she was
in good condition. which I must
say is a credit to your mother
she looks after you well. Love
                              Dad

Wednesday 5th April 1939
Christine has her first holiday
from school it is Easter holidays

Friday April 7th Good Friday 1939
Mussolini The Dictator of Italy
in Oct invaded Albiania Albania
Things are in a terriable state
we do not no which way thing
are going to turn out.
                              Love Dad

20 March 1939

Christine has got a touch of flue, Mother has kept her away from school for this week, I hope she will be better soon.
Love Dad.

—

28 March 1939

Christine examined by the Doctor @ the school, he said she was in good condition, which I must say is a credit to your Mother, she looks after you well.
Love Dad.

—

5 April 1939

Christine has her first holiday from school, it is Easter holidays.

—

7 April 1939 – Good Friday

Mussolini the Dictator of Italy invaded Albania. Things are in a terriable state, we do not no which way things are going to turn out.
Love Dad.

—

10 April 1939

We all went to Herne Bay for the Easter, we had a good time, Christine is there for the rest of the week with Mother.
Love Dad.

—

17 April 1939

We had a letter from school asking us if we would consent to Christine being Evacuated in the event of war. We said no, we are going to keep you with us.
Love Dad.

—

28 May 1939

Took Christine for the day to Eastbourne, we had a good day and we booked up our holidays there.
Love Dad.

—

7 June 1939

Christine had her teeth examined @ school, they told Mother that your teeth were alright.
Love Dad.

—

8 July 1939

Christine went with us to Herne Bay for week end, we had a good time. Before we went Christine put umbrella in her mouth and could not get it out untill Mother done it for her.

Love Dad.

—

22 July 1939

We took Christine to Eastbourne with us for our holidays, we had a very good time, on the Sunday we went to Beachy Head. Monday we went to Brighton and saw aunt Lottie and family. Tuesday we went a long to the Crumble's, Wednesday to Hastings & St Leonard's and the rest of the week we kept in Eastbourne. Christine had a very bad Boil on her backside, had to use boil plaster on it, otherwise every thing was o.k.

Love Dad.

—

6 August 1939

Percy and Cyril came up to London for a week's holiday. Christine went with them to Chiswick Empire and saw a play called a Little bit of Fluff.

—

Aug 24th 1939

Dear Christine @ the time
of writing this there is
another crisis, this time
it is between Poland
and Germany it looks
very much as if there will
be a war before the
week is out. so if ~~war~~
does come. always remember
that I will always love
you and your mother
to my last day of my
Life, so always stick to
your mother and do as
she tells you.

Love Dad

13 August 1939

Christine and Mother went to Herne Bay for a week and took Beryl with them. They had a good time.
Love Dad.

—

24 Aug 1939

Dear Christine
@ the time of writing this there is another Crisis, this time it is between Poland and Germany, it looks very much as if there will be a war before the week is out, so if war does come always remember that I will always love you and your Mother to my last day of my life, so always stick to your Mother and do as she tells you.
Love Dad.

—

29 August 1939

Mother took Christine away to Eastbourne to see if it would be all right for them there in case war came but Mother could not stand it and came home. All school children are being evacuated to morrow Friday 1st Aug 1939 but we are sending you and Mother too Harold and Fay's @ Hounslow. Things look very bad.
Love Dad.

—

Friday 1 Sept 1939

Christine & Mother went to
Hanworth to Harold & Fays
for Safety

Friday 1st Sept 1939
Germany invaded Poland

Sunday Sept 3rd 1939
Great Britian & France
declared War on Germany
@ 11 oclock in the Morning

Friday 8th Sept 1939
Christine & Mother came Back
from Hanworth to be home
with me   love Dad

1 September 1939

Christine & Mother went to Hanworth to Harold and Fays for safety.

—

Germany invaded Poland.

—

3 September 1939

Great Britain and France declared War on Germany @ 11 oclock in the Morning.

—

8 September 1939

Christine & Mother came Back from Hanworth to be home with me.
Love Dad.

—

17 September 1939

Russia invaded Poland.

—

25 September 1939

The war has now been on for 4 weeks and Poland has been smashed to pieces but they are a gallant little country and are still Fighting to the Last man which they said they would do, God help them.
Love Dad.

—

14 October 1939

Christine went to Eva's Wedding, did not enjoy it very much.
Love Dad.

—

18 October 1939

Christine had a boil on her backside, she had one there befor but it was on the other side, it is all better now.
Love Dad.

—

3 November 1939

Christine went to Barbara's birthday party, she was one year old, you had a good time.
Love Dad.

—

Sunday 17 Sept 1939
Russia invaded Poland

Monday Sept 25th 1939
. The war has now been on
for 4 Weeks and Poland has
been smashed to pieces but
they are a gallant little
country country and are
still Fighting to the Last
man which they said they
would do, God Help them
                    Love Dad

Saturday 14th October 1939
Christine Went to Eva's
Wedding did not enjoy it
every much.
                    Love Dad

1 November 1939

Christine can tell the time, you are only 5 years old.

—

30 November 1939

Christine went to be examined by doctor for her to be evacuated and was passed fit. You are to go on Saturday 2nd Dec 1939.
Love Dad.

—

30 November 1939

Russia has invaded Finland, they are bombing the women and children.
Love Dad.

—

1 December 1939

We have made up our minds not to send Christine away, we are going to keep her with us as we cannot part with her, the trouble is we love her to much to let her go to be looked after by other people.
With love from your Mother and dad.

—

Friday 1st Dec 1939
we have made up our minds
not to send christine away
we are going to keep her with
us as we cannot part with
her, the trouble is we love
her to much to let her go
to be looked after by other
people with love from your
Mother and dad

Sunday 31st Dec 1939

we all went to church this
after-noon for old year out
& new year in ~~service~~ service
we had to go early this year
on account of the Black out.
We have had another good
year christine & we hope it
will be as good in 1940
@ the time of writing the
crountry has call up all men
to the age 27 so my time
is not far off but we hope
it will be all over befor
then. If I do have to go stick
fast to your Mother she is a good
one to you. Love from
                              Dad

31 December 1939

We all went to church this after-noon for old year out
& new year in service, we had to go early this year on
account of the Black out. We have had another good year
Christine & we hope it will be as good in 1940. @ the
time of writing the Crountry has call up all men to the
age 27 so my time is not far off but we hope it will be
all over befor then. If I do have to go stick fast to your
Mother, she is a good one to you.
Love from Dad.

—

1940

20 February 1940

Dear Christine

Many things have happened since I last wrote in this Book in regards to the war. But the funniest was when Hitler made a speech in Germany and he said he was going to be King of England in April 20th and this cartoon came out the next day.

Love Dad.

At time of writing you have a nasty cold, but we hope it will be better soon.

—

13 March 1940

The war ended with Russia and Finland after many lives had been lost, Finland gave in much to my regret.

—

20 March 1940

Christine,

Went to the doctors about her colds, you seem to get one then catch another, the doctor said that you had a catarrh.

9 April 1940

Germany invaded Norway & Denmark. Denmark did not resist but Norway is fighting back & we are going to her aid.

—

10 May 1940

Germany Invaded Holland & Belgium.

—

10 June 1940

Italy declarded war on England & France.

—

8 July 1940

Mother Brought a new bed for Christine as she was getting to big for her cot, it has upset Mother a bit as it is the last bit of Christine child hood days but we are not getting rid of it, we are going to keep it untill you get a big girl.
All my love, Dad.

—

Christine with Billie the cat who was rescued from the rubble of the bombsite one week after the bombing.

9 October 1940

Dear Christine

A lot has happened since I last wrote in this book. We had a time bombe @ the back of our shelter, we had to be evacuated from our home but we are back home again now. But all us people in London now do is to sleep in our shelters. The sirens have just gone which is 7 oclock and we will be here untill 6 oclock next morning but you can take it from me Christine we have a rough time. Love Dad.

—

7 November 1940

Dear Christine
A lot has happened since I wrote in this Book last, you have been away to Doncaster for this last 3 weeks & I can tell you I have never missed you so much in all my life. I don't think that I could stand another 3 weeks like it, it might sound funny coming from me but you can take it from me you are every thing in the world to me so God bless you & I hope he will take you through this awful war so good night my Dear.
Love Daddy.

—

11 December 1940

Dear Christine
This is one of the saddess days of my life. Your Gran-Mar Pierce died at 7.15 Wednesday night after 4 weeks illness she die of cancer in the stomach and I can say she was a Grand old lady age 74, so good night my dear and I hope that we can pull through this war together.
Love Daddy.

—

May 10th 1940
Germany Invaded
  Holland & Belgium

_____   _____

Monday 10 June 1940

Italy declared war on
England & France

Monday 9a
Monday July 8th 1940

Mother Brought a New bed
for christine as she was getting
to big for her cot, it has upset
Mother a bit as it is the
Last bit of christine child Hood
days but we are not getting

kid of it we are going to keep
it untill you get a big girl
all my hove . dad.

—————————————

Wednesday 9 Oct 1940
Dear Christine
a lot has happened since I last
wrote in this book. We
had a time bombe @ the back
of our shelter we had to be
evacuated from our home but we
are back home again now.
But all the people in London
now do is to sleep in our
shelters. The sirens have just gone
which is 7 oclock and we will
be here until 6 oclock next
morning but you can take
it from me Christine we
have a rough time. Love
            dad

Tuesday 31 Dec 1940

Dear Christine

This is the end of
1940 + I must say it has been
a very bad year indeed in regards
of the War. We were evacuated
from our home on account of a time
bomb that night was the worst
night we had you slept all through
it. next time we had all the
windows of the house blown out
and we have been sleeping in
a Shelter, but these last few
nights it has been to cold. At this
present we are making the Italians
run for their Lives.
                    Good night Daddy

31 December 1940

Dear Christine

This is the end of 1940 & I must say it has been a very bad year indeed in regards of the War. We were evacuated from our home on account of a time bombe, that night was the worst night we had, you slept all through it. Next time we had all the windows of the house blown out and we have been sleeping in a Shelter, but these last few nights it has been to cold. At this presant we are making the Italians run for there lives.

Good night Daddy.

—

1941

4 January 1941

Gran-Ma Morris had a Telegram from Uncle Tom to say
Auntie Dorothy has given birth to a baby boy, Can't say if it
was born on Friday the 3 or Sat 4th untill we see Uncle Tom.
Best love Daddy.
At this moment Christine you are sitting by my side.
P.S. Baby was born Thursday Jan 2nd at 12.30 P.M.

—

11 January 1941

Dear Christine
I went Sat 11 Jan to register for Military Service. I have
asked to go in the R.A.F.
Love Dad.

—

11 February 1941

Dear Christine
We had you Inoculated against Diphtheria as a lot of
children die with it, so you see Mother has had it done.
So you can see she looks after you well.
Love Dad.

Wednesday 12th March 1941

Dear Christine

I went up for My Medical
examination and was Graded
Grade III on account of my right
eye, so it looks as if I shall
be staying at home, I am very
pleased in one way because I
can stay with you & Mother.
At this presant moment we are
going through bad raids &
you are very good while they
are on, Heres hoping we can
pull through to the end
                Love
                     Dad

12 March 1941

Dear Christine

I went up for my medical examination and was Graded Grade III on account of my right eye, so it looks as if I shall be staying at home, I am very pleased in one way because I can stay with you & Mother. At this presant moment we are going through bad raids & you are very good while they are on, here's hoping we can pull through to the end.

Love Dad.

—

27 March 1941

Dear Christine

You have been unlucky & caught the scabies, it is a nasty complaint, it is picked up off other people.

You see oweing to the life we have had to live through air raids it could had been caught in the public shelter where we have been going to or else at school. You can take it from me it is no fault of your Mother's, as she has all ways kept you so very clean but Mother is very worryed about it, we have given you three sul [salt?] baths & another one to morrow & we hope it will be all gone.

Will close now as you are waiting for me to play with you.

Good night my love, Dad.

—

29 March 1941

Dear Christine
I have just had my papers sent to me to fill in to go in the munition factory, hope I can get out of it so I can look after you & Mother.
Love Dad.

—

16 April 1941

Dear Christine
Last night was the worst that we have had to go through in regards to Air Raids, it started at 9.00 & went on untill 5.0 oclock next morning & Air Plains were over all the time & they have done a lot of damage, our house suffered quite a lot, it was done by Land Mine. The whole of King St shops were a proper wrecks next morning. I hope that we do not have to go through another night like it. Our Air Men went to Berlin last night & gave them a taste of there own medicine.
With lots of love from Dad & Mother.

—

8 June 1941

Dear Christine
We all went to Uncle Tom's place at Walton on Thames for the Christening of baby James, which was at 4 oclock at Walton church, he was a very good baby & never cryed at all & a very nice time we had except Mother who's

feet were very Bad & she could not walk.
Love Dad.

—

23 June 1941

Dear Christine
I started my holidays, we did not go away on account of the war and air raids. But we had a nice time just the same. We went to Hampton Court on Monday by Boat, very nice trip.

—

24 June 1941

We went to Windsor & that is where you first started to swim & I was very pleased with your first attempt.

—

25 June 1941

We went to Maidenhead, it was a nice Day & we enjoyed it.

—

26 June 1941

We went to Staines & you had another go at swimming in the swimming Pool & you done very well.

—

27 June 1941

We went to Windsor again & you had another swim.

—

28 June 1941

We done our shopping & went to the pictures.
Love Dad.

—

17 July 1941

Today is Christine birthday & you had Barbara to tea, you had a nice time & plenty of money presants as other things were so expenesive to buy.
Love Dad.

—

29 July 1941

Christine & Mother went away for a 2 weeks holiday to Gilford, you stayed at Lord Darrington Country House. I will be coming down to see you Sunday 3rd, hope you have a good time.
Love Dad.

—

14 October 1941

Dear Christine

The war at this very moment is raging in Russia where they are fighting for there very lives & the Blood shed there is un-speakable, the Jerrys are getting a bit more than they asked for, the fighting is raging around Moscow which is the capital and we are all praying that the Russians can keep them out side, so they will get the full blast of the winter. While this war has been on old Jerry has left us alone in London and we are all hoping that they don't start again.

Love Dad.

—

10 December 1941

Christine went to the school dentist to have her teeth looked at so you be having two out very soon, you have had the tooth ache lately, will let you no later.

Love Daddy.

—

31 December 1941

Uncle Alf came home on a 48 hours leave and had the old year out and new year in with us.

Love Dad.

—

Dear Christine

This is the end of the year 1941, and I must say that we have been through quite a lot togeather, and we must thank the <u>Lord Almighty</u> for our safety. We have had some near misses with bombes from Jerry, but the tide is turning and Jerry is getting a nasty hiding from the Russians & our men in Libya. I must say that all through these Raids you have been a very brave girl.

All my best love,

From Dad.

—

Dear Christine this is the end
of the year 1941, and I must
say that we have been through
quite a lot togeather,
and we must thank the <u>Lord</u>
<u>Almighty</u> for our safty, We have
had some near misses with
bombes from Jerry, but the
tide is turning and Jerry
is getting a nasty hiding
from the Russians + our men
in Libya. I must say that
all through these Raids you
have been a very brave girl

   All my best Love

      From Dad

1942

2 January 1942

Christine went to the dentist to have her teeth out, you had two by gas, it has upset your tummy a bit so we have put you to bed early.
Love Dad.
A good start for 1942, my love.

—

29 January 1942

Christine bought Mother a pair of silk stockings for her birthday, Mother was 30 years of age.
Love Daddy.

—

19 March 1942

Dear Christine
Uncle Harold went into the Army today in the R.A.S.C. He has got to go to Wiltshire.

At this very moment the Russian are fighting the Jerrys very hard and are driving them back, we have got a lot to thank them for.
Love Dad.

5 April 1942

Christine starts to learn to roller skate.

After 3 times going out on them she can go by her self, & after a week you were very good indeed, I take her out every night for half an hour. After you have got very good and can do some tricks on them, I am going to put you on the Ice to do Ice skating which is my one desire to see you do your stuff on the Ice. I pull your leg and call you Skating Fanny but I must say you do enjoy it.
Love Daddy.

—

26 May 1942

Dear Christine
You have just caught the Chicken Pox, you must have caught it from your girl friends, you have all been practising for a concert, first one got it then another so altogeother there were six of you so they have had to cancell the concert untill you are all better. You have to stay at home for three week.
Love Daddy.

—

20 June 1942

Dear Christine
We had our holidays but we were not able to go away but we did go to Bognor Regis for one day, all the Front was

bared [barbed] wires so we could not go on the Sands.
That was Monday.

Tues we went to Richmond.

Wednesday we went to Guilford.

Thursday we went to Windsor.

Friday   "   "   " Richmond with Barbara.

Sat to the AAA Sports Meeting and @ night to a show so
that finish our holiday.
Love Daddy.

—

26 June 1942

Dear Christine
Things are not going very well with the war, we have
lost a big Battle in Libya & 23,000 of our men have
been taken Prisoners & now the Battle of Egypt has just
started we are all hoping we can make a stand there &
hold them, will write more later.
Love Daddy.

—

17 July 1942

Dear Christine
Today is your birthday & I must say you had a very good
time indeed, Mother worked very hard & made cakes &
mince pies & every thing you could eat, you would not

Friday 26 June 1942

Dear Christine !!

Things are not going very
well with the war we have Lost
a big Battle in Libya & 23 000
of our men have been taken
Prisoners & now the Battle of Egypt
has Just started we are all hoping
we can make a stand there &
hold them will write more later
Love Daddy

Friday 17 . July 1942
Dear Christine
        To day is your birthday & I must
say you had a very good time indeed
mother worked very hard & made cakes
& mince pies + every thing you could
eat you would. not think there was
a war on. As a matter of fact Hitler
sent his Bombers over + the Sirens
went Just as you were having your
party that was 4·30 + it was the
fast time we'd her them in months
But since then we have had them
6 times this week but no Bombs near
us. We close now
                    love Daddy

think there was a war on. As a matter of fact Hitler sent his Bombers over & the Sirens went just as you were having your party that was 4.30 & it was the first time we'd her [heard] them in months. But since then we have had them 6 times this week but no Bombs near us. We close now.

Love Daddy.

—

11 August 1942

Dear Christine

We went to a sports meeting belonging to Lyons at Sudbury & we had a very Good time, all it cost was 1/6 that included a very nice tea & show, after that there was dancing, this was your first big dance & you danced well. Walzts [Waltz] & you done the Veleta, got home at 11.30.

Love Daddy.

—

26 September 1942

Christine you went to your first big dance, at Oxford Corner House which belongs to Lyons, it is very flash, there you had several dances and we had quite a good evening.

Love Daddy.

—

27 September 1942

Well Christine I have kept my promise to you regarding Ice skating, we went Sunday and you done very well indeed, you went on your own & then some lady came and took you round & you went round with her very good so he's hoping for next time which will be this Sunday.

My best love, Daddy.

—

15 November 1942

Dear Christine

Today is a Great day for rejoucing, the church bells were rang all over the crountry to announce the Victory of our 8th Army in Egypt. Our Boys are smashing the Germans back & they are on the run which is great news for us, also today is your Granddad's birthday, more news later.

Love Daddy.

—

27 November 1942

Auntie Dorothy has had another baby boy, since it was born it has been on the danger list, it has yellow Jaundice, the Doctor did not expect it to live, Mummy and Nanna keep going to see how it is going along, it is much about the same now. Will let you know later how it gets along.

Love Daddy.

be this Sunday
        My best Love
            Daddy

Sunday 15 November 1942
Dear Christine
            Today is a Great day
for rejoicing, the church bells
were rang all over the ~~croun cun~~
crountryto announce the Victory
of our 8th Army in Egypt. Our
Boys are smashing the Germans
back & they are on the run
which is great news for us, also
today is your Granddad's birthday
more news later

            Love Daddy

1943

10 January 1943

Christine you took part in Tableaux at church, is was to do with the Life of Jesus, you were a page, Mother & I came to see it, is was very good.
Love Daddy.

—

7 January 1943

We went with Christine to a tea & small concert at your Brownies, you gave a turn or too & done very well.

You were presented with a star by your captain for First class attendance.
Love Daddy.

—

16 January 1943

Dear Christine
Last night our Boys went and bombed Berlin & started some big Fires.

—

Thursday 7 Jan 1943
we went with christine to
a tea + small concert at your
Brownies you gave a turn or
too + done very well
you were presented with a star
by your captain for first class
attendance
Love Daddy

Saturday 16 Jan 1943
Dear christine
Last night our Boys went and
bombed Berlin + started some big Fires

Sunday 17 Jan 1943
so Jerry came over here tonight
started at 8-20 untill 10 o'clock the gunfire
was Heavy you have Just gone to bed
Love Daddy

17 January 1943

So Jerry came over here tonight, started at 8.20 untill 10 oclock, the gunfire was Heavy, you have just gone to bed. Love Daddy.

—

20 January 1943

Dear Christine
Some German Raiders came over this morning & dropped bombs on a school, there was 45 children found dead up till now & 12 more still missing, the school was @ Lewisham.
Love Daddy.

—

4 March 1943

Mother has not been very well this last two weeks, had the flue & it has left her with a lot of trouble with her ear noises that was getting her down. So if at any time you have trouble with your ears go to the doctor's at once, don't touch them yourself.
Love Daddy.

—

10 March 1943   Wednesday

Dear christine

Your Auntie Eileen gave
birth to a baby girl she was
born at Grove Road Hospital
Richmond Auntie is going to
call it Daphne Sylvia

Love Daddy

Monday 29th of March 1943

Dear Christine

General Montgomery who is in
charge of our 8th Army has
smashed his way through
the Mareth line which the
Germans held, this is a big
Victory for us.

Love Daddy

10 March 1943

Dear Christine
Your Auntie Eileen gave birth to a baby girl she was born at Grove Road Hospital, Richmond. Auntie is going to call it Daphne Sylvia.
Love Daddy.

—

29 March 1943

General Montgomery who is in charge of our 8th Army has smashed he's way through the Mareth Line which the Germans held, this is a big Victory for us.
Love Daddy.

—

26 March 1943

Dear Christine
Your Uncle Alf can [came] home on leave for 11 days before going oversea's, we had a good time togeather. Uncle went back on Monday 5th of April we all went up to the Station with him, the train left at 9.20 P.M. & it was very upseting to see them go so let us pray to God he will come back to us all safely.
Love Daddy.

—

6 April 1943

Dear Christine
Our 8th Army have won another big Victory north of Gabes, we have taken 6,000 prisoners, I hope our luck will hold.
Love Daddy.

—

29 April 1943

Dear Christine
Your grandad Morris had to go to hospital for internal trouble and he has been very bad, Nanna is worried because she thinks he has not got much longer to go. Will let you know more later.
Love Daddy.

—

12 May 1943

Dear Christine
@ 8.15 last night the fighting in North Africa has ended, the Germans & Italians have been bashed to bits, up to now there are 150,000 prisoners, 250 Tanks, 1,000 Guns & lot more stuff to come in. This Cartoon is what was published after the battle. Alexander was the General in charge of the men in the field with Montgomery & Anderson.
Love Daddy.

21 May 1943

Dear Christine
Your Grandad Morris was taken ill during the night, I had to go & fetch the doctor at 3 oclock in the morning & he was sent to hospital, he was taken to Du-Cane-Road at 4.30 A.M.

—

26 May 1943

Dear Christine
Your Grandad Morris has had some kind of an operation to day, they have put some tubes inside him to drain him out but I think the big operation is to come, will let you know more later.
Love Daddy.

—

30 May 1943

Christine
You started going to music lesson so we are hoping you will do good at it, It will come in handy to you when you get older.
Love Daddy.

—

15 June 1943

Christine

A German airoplain came over last night & dropped bombs & one was very close to us, we thought it was our last, it came so near Mother & I dropped on the bedroom floor beside your bed thinking it was going to hit us but we were lucky, so here's hoping we remain lucky untill it is all over.

Love Daddy.

—

9 July 1943

Dear Christine

The British troops & Canadian with American troops have invaded Sicily, it started at 10.15 on Friday with Air Bourne troops but the real invasion started at 3 oclock on the Saturday morning, up till now things are going well, will let you know more later.

Love Daddy.

2,000 Boats took part.

—

17 July 1943

Christine Birthday.
All Best Wishes.
Love Daddy & Mother.

—

Cartoon depicts the variety of forces involved in the Battle of Tunis including the armies of General Alexander, General Montgomery and General Anderson.

28 July 1943

Dear Christine

Your Grandad Morris past away at 10.20, he was in Duncane Hospital, Hammersmith. He had suffered great pain but had a peacefull end. He's illness was caused through Cancer of Bowl [bowel] and Bladder, he was also Blind. The funeral will be on Tuesday 3rd of August. Love Daddy.

—

3 August 1943

Dear Christine
Your Grandad Morris was buried today Hammersmith
Cemetry, Mortlake.
Love Daddy.

—

9 August 1943

Dear Christine
We went on our holidays to Herne Bay we did not
think they would let us pass the station as it was a band
[banned] area but we got through and stayed for the
week and we had a good time, we took Nanna Morris
with us, the guns were going most of the day but we
were us't to them.
Love Daddy.

—

Dear Christine
The invasion of Sicily which I wrote about a little way
back is all over, we had beaten the Germans again and it
was another Dunkirk for them, there is another big move
coming off. Will let you know as soon as it happens.
Love Daddy.

—

3 September 1943

Dear Christine
British & 8th Army & Canadian troops invaded Italy this morning at 3.45 A.M. everything is going well will let you know more later.
Love Daddy.

—

8 September 1943

Dear Christine
I have great news for you, the Italian Government has given in and excepted [accepted] our terms of unconditional surrender so Italy is now out of the war, now for the Germans.
Love Daddy.

—

13 October 1943

Dear Christine
Italy has declared War on Germany, it seems strange as Italy & the Germans were dear old pals.
    Will let you know more later.
Love Daddy.

—

1944

1 January 1944

Dear Christine

The old year has gone & I must say that we had a very good year considering that the war is still on. But 1943 has left us with greate Victorys & I might say the turning point of the war, only last night the R.A.F. dropped 1,000 tons of bombs on Berlin & our boys are waiting to invade & they are saying that this year will be the last of this war, I hope so.

Our Christmas Dinner was chicken, 3 lumps of Pork, Christmas pudding, mince pies, not bad after nearly 5 years of war.
Love Daddy.

—

13 January 1944

Dear Christine

I thought you would like to have this Clothing Book of yours as it would be something to look at in years to come. We had just had an Air Raid Warning but nothing happened.
Love Daddy.

—

Thursday 13 January 1944

Dear Christine

    I thought you would like to have this Clothing Book of your's as it would be something to look at in years to come. We have just had an Air Raid Warning but nothing happened

                Love Daddy

1942-43 CLOTHING BOOK

This book may not be used until the holder's name, full postal address and National Registration (Identity Card) Number have been plainly written below IN INK.

NAME (BLOCK LETTERS) PIERCE. C.S.

ADDRESS (BLOCK LETTERS) 33 CAMBRIDGE. GROVE

(TOWN) HAMMERSMITH   (COUNTY) MIDD'X

NATIONAL REGISTRATION (IDENTITY CARD) NUMBER

AJOU / 290 / 3

Read the instructions within carefully, and take great care not to lose this book

Page 1

Clothing was so restricted that it was impossible to purchase without the clothing book. Christine was taught to memorise her identity card number as a very small child.

6 February 1944

Dear Christine

Uncle Alf got married to-day to Eva Green, we all went to the wedding and had a nice time.

Love Daddy.

—

20 February 1944

Dear Christine

We had a very bad air raid last night, it is one of the worst we have had round the District H.E. and time bombs but I prayed to God to take us safely through & he did. We wish this war would end as it is just as bad for the German people as it is for us.

Love Daddy.

—

23 February 1944

Dear Christine

Last night the Germans came over & raided London & we had a bad night. Bombs dropped all round us & I am sorry to say that your great Aunt Ada was killed this night & her daughter was trapped for 22 hours & she was got out alive but her husband was killed also.

Love Daddy.

—

2 March 1944

Dear Christine
Your Aunt Ada was buried today and her Son-in-Law at Fulham Cemetry, East Sheen.
Love Daddy.

—

6 April 1944

Dear Christine
Your Uncle Geoff went into the army today, he was 41, sent to Bradford in Yorkshire, I do not know what regiment he is going into yet.
Love Daddy.

—

5 June 1944

Dear Christine
Our troops of the 8th Army and American 5th Army have entered Rome the capital of Italy, it is a greate Victory for us. We have taken over 20,000 prisoners and we are still driving the Germans back, the General in charge is Alexander.
Love Daddy.

—

Wednesday Febuary 23rd 1944

Dear Christine

Last night the Germans came over
+ raided london + we had a
bad night. bombs dropped all
round us + I am sorry to say
that your great Aunt Ada was
killed this Night + her daughter
was trapped for 22 hours
+ she was got out alive.
but her husband was killed
also.

       Love Daddy.

Thursday 2 March 1944

Dear Christine

your Aunt Ada Was buried
today And her Son-in-Law
at Fulham Cemetery East Sheen

       Love Daddy

6 June 1944

Dear Christine
To day is the biggest day in our history, our Armys have landed in France, there were over 4,000 ships took part and over 11,000 aircraft, the landing took place @ 6.00 clock this morning, the airbourne troops landed first & I think your Uncle Alf is in it, will let you know more as news comes in.
Love Daddy.

—

23 June 1944

Dear Christine
Last night was the worst night we have been through. Gerry sent one of pilot less plains over & Bombed our home flat to the Ground, we were very luck that your Mother & myself were not killed, but we must thank God, he was watching over us & took us safely through so we will have to make a new home after the war, I must say you were very Brave right through.

  Good night, love, God Bless you,
Love Daddy.

—

Tuesday June 6th 1944

Dear Christine

to day is the biggest day in our
history our Armys have landed
in France there were over 4,000
ships took part and over 11,000
aircraft, the landing took place
@ 6.00 clock this morning, the
airbourne troops landed first &
I think your Uncle Alf is in
it will let you know more as
news comes to in.

      Love Daddy

17 July 1944

Dear Christine
Today is your birthday & what a day you have had, we held your party on the old Bomb sit [site] of our home & the Daily Mirror reporter cam down & took photos of it, we are waiting for the paper to come out, every body had a wonderful time, you had 17 cards and lots of money presents, also you were a very good girl & very helpful, the flybombs are still coming over.
Good Bye,
Love Daddy.

—

1 August 1944

Dear Christine
This month has been the best we have had in this war, we have driven the Germans out of Normandy & France & are into Holland & B and we are just about to start the Battle of Germany, we let you know more later on.
Love Daddy.

—

2 September 1944

Uncle Harold went to France, will let you know more later.
Love Daddy.

—

Christine's tenth birthday party. A wonderful display of the spirit of
Londoners following a bombing disaster.

Another picture of the party.

7 September 1944

Dear Christine
Uncle Alf came back from France safe & sound.
Love Daddy.

—

8 September 1944

Dear Christine
The Germans are sending Rockets over at us now as well as fly bombs, the first one dropped at Chiswich & the second one at Kew & we have had a lot more since. They are worse than the fly bombs because you can't hear the coming. We still go to the shelter at night.
Love Daddy.

—

27 November 1944

We bought a piano for Christine for £30-0-0 & we have got a good bargain.
Love Daddy.

—

12 December 1944

Christine had a air Graph from Italy from a stranger wishing her a merry Xams [Xmas], she is going to answer it.
Love Daddy.

Dear Christine Aug 1st 1944

This month has been the best
we have had I in this war
we have driven the Germans
out of Normandy & France
& are into Holland + B
and We are Just about to
Start the Battle of Germany
we let you know more
later on

       Love Daddy

Sat 2nd September 1944
Uncle Harold went to
France will let you know
more later

       Love Daddy

1945

8 January 1945

Dear Christine

At the time of writing this letter there is a big battle going on, the Germanys have broken through the American lines & the British have been rush up to stop them. Well your Uncle Alf is in that battle they are call Montgomerys Devil. This cutting from the paper will tell you all.

Love Daddy.

Christine's mother's brother, Alfred Morris, served in the Sixth Airborne Division – 'A Red Devil'.

Dear Christine   8ᵗʰ Jan 1945
at the time of writing this letter
there is a big battle going on
the Germanys have broken through
the American lines + the British
have been rush up to stop them
Well your Uncle Alf is in that
battle they are call Montgomerys
Devil. this cutting from the paper
will tell you all
        Love Daddy

MONTY'S RED DEVILS ARE THERE

Played a Big Part

The British Sixth Airborne Division, the "Red Devils," are fighting in the Ardennes as part of the British force thrown in to plug the German breakthrough. They played a big part in the capture of Bure.

The men of the Sixth Division were about to eat their Christmas dinner when their orders came. An officer told me: "We were simply told 'You'll be in the Ardennes to-morrow. Within three days of the first word we were at grips with the Germans."

CANADIANS, TOO

Canadian troops are fighting with Field Marshal Montgomery on the Ardennes front, Berlin radio said this afternoon. The announcer reported: "All attacks by Canadian forces east of Marche failed."

14 February 1945

Dear Christine

Today is a very sad day again for us, the Germans who are firing rockets at us dropped one very near us, it shook the life out of this Place, you were in bed, Mother was sitting by the fire & the rocket came, it was 10 oclock at night, well my love it came & fell on your Uncle Fred's home & killed him & your Auntie Mary, Cousin Peter, Jean & the baby, it wiped the whole family out. We hope that we pull safely through as we have gone through enough already.

Love Daddy.

—

24 February 1945

Dear Christine

Your Cousin Joan got married to day to an American officer in the 8th Air Force, you were to have been her brides maid but owing to your Uncle Fred's Family waiting to be buried you could not be it, but we went to the party and had a nice time in a quite [quiet] way. Joanie was only 18 years old.

Love Daddy.

—

25 February 1945

Your Uncle Alf has just this minute come home from Holland from the Battle front, he will be coming round here tonight.
Love Daddy.

—

26 February 1945

Your Uncle Fred's Family was buried today at Hammersmith Cemetery.
Love Daddy.

—

8 May 1945

Dear Christine
This day is the greatest in our history, the War is over with Germany, we have beaten them to there knees & God has answered our prayers & taken us safely through. We have been to the Hammersmith Broadway singing & dancing, it is something you will not forget & that as gone on for all the week until 1 & 2 in the morning.
Love Daddy.

—

15. 2. 45.   7535778 PTE GRANT C. R.A.M.C.
                  9th Ind. C.C.S.
                  C. M. F.

Dear Miss Pierie,
            Thank you ever so
much for your nice letter and wishes,
I shall try to explain matters in
my next few lines.
    You must believe me when I say
that I did not think you a Blonde
of eighteen, nor a girl of ten, but
a kind old Lady who happened
to send along some papers to a
few weary soldiers.
    They were welcomed with open
arms, and I took it upon myself
to thank you in some way. I
wanted at first to write, but chang-
ed my mind and only sent the
X'mas greetings without explain-
ing anything. Your address
was written in ink on one of them.

An 'air graph' from the 'stranger' Cedric Grant in response to Christine's letter.

I hope I have not annoyed you by writing, and any bother caused, and ask your forgiveness.

I'm not in the middle East but in Italy and had quite a nice time during X'mas & New Year, am pleased to hear that you didn't do bad yourself, but as you must know, even if ten years old that there's nothing like home, and I join with you in wishing that this Year brings no peace, and a place where little girls like you can live without fear in a free world.

Thanks once again for every thing including the papers.

With my best wishes,

Cedric Grant.

First fold here

13 May 1945

Dear Christine
We went to the Strand in London to see the King &
Queen, you had a good view of the Princess, King Peter
& the King of Norway, King of Denmark, Queen Mary
& Mr Churchill.
Love Daddy.

—

21 June 1945

Dear Christine
This cutting from the paper showes you what the
Londoners went through during the bombing of London
which you were in all the time.

—

11 July 1945

Dear Christine
You had to go to the Godolphine High School for girls
for an entrance test because you done well in your schol-
arship & you passed there test, you start school there on
Sept 13th 1945. Good luck Christine, do your best.
Love Daddy.

—

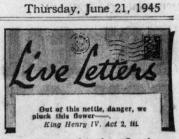

Thursday, June 21, 1945

Live Letters

Out of this nettle, danger, we pluck this flower——.
King Henry IV. Act 2, iii.

Letter from an American Gentleman

From Mr. J. R. CRANE, an American now over here:

YOUR paper will, I know, assist me in paying tribute to the people of London—the world's mightiest people. I am an American soldier, soon to leave this great city for another theatre of war, but I will take with me everlasting memories and pictures of an unconquerable race.

I shall remember, always, the faces of two little children in Stepney, who shepherded my panic-stricken body into a shelter as a flying-bomb shattered houses and human flesh into a pulp not fifty yards away; of a pianist in a public-house, in a side street off your bomb-splattered Lambeth Walk, whose rhythm on the keys offered a challenge to the hate and fury of yet another savage Hitler onslaught to break the backbone of the tough London populace.

I shall remember Mr. and Mrs. X, of Brixton, who made me share the comforts of their modest house on my days of leave; and Edna, my London sweetheart, who, until unseen death in the form of a rocket took her from me was to become my wife.

If I survive th next episode in the quest for peace, and return home, I shall always say to myself—" The debt the world owes to you people of London will never be paid. It cannot be paid. The price is too high. God bless you all."

To you, Mr. Crane, who, because of a London blitz, must now walk alone, we say only, "Thank you and God bless."

This has been described as 'an eye opener which gave a good idea of what the Americans thought of us'.

2 December 1945

Your Uncle Alf was Demobbed from the Army so he came through safely, after what he had to go through it is amazing.
Love Daddy.

Sunday 9 Dec 1945

Christine you wore your first
pair of stockings today today
you feel quite beg about it
        Love Daddy

Sunday 16 Dec 1945
    Christine was confirmed by the
Bishop of London at St John's
Church Hammersmith
        Love Daddy

4th May Tuesday 1946
    Dear Christine
We went to a dance @ the new Town
Hall Hammersmith it was a Gaumont
Studio dance & you and myself won
the spot dance the prize was two
8/6 ticket for the pictures
        Love Daddy

9 December 1945

Christine you wore your first pair of stockings today, you feel quite big about it.
Love Daddy.

—

16 December 1945

Christine was confirmed by the Bishop of London at St John's Church, Hammersmith.
Love Daddy.

—

Postscript

I should like to pay tribute to both my parents who worked hard to bring me up in very difficult times. In spite of the trauma we lived through, I have very happy memories: two wonderful parents who loved each other and me, and who kept cheerful throughout all the troubles and hardship. I was a lucky little girl and I loved them both very much. They were proud of me, and I am so proud of them.

There are two uncanny coincidences to my story. As a reward for passing my exams to get into the Godolphin and Latymer School, my parents went to a well-known London jeweller to buy me a watch, which I still have to this day, that bears the jeweller's name, Camerer Cuss. What my parents did not know was that many years later I would marry the jeweller's son.

The second coincidence on that day was that as my father stood in the shop, he did not know that during 1940–45 the jeweller Frank Cuss and his wife had shown great kindness to two teenage refugees from Belgium. In 1996, over fifty years later, one of the 'Belgian boys', then aged 80, took my husband and I to Ypres, and by chance we discovered my father's brother Bill's name on the Menin Gate, lost without trace, a fact that was unknown to any of my family. As a result of this discovery, we returned to the Menin Gate on 6 June 1997 to commemorate the eightieth anniversary of the death of my father's brother,

William Pierce. There happened to be a piper and drummer and speeches that evening. The bugles were played and I laid a wreath of poppies. Uncle Bill had an honourable funeral at last.

In Memory of my Father

A Father's Love is precious, very tender, very dear.
To know that you are special and that he is always near.
Dad taught me how to ride a bike, he taught me how to skate,
And if I ever needed him, I never had to wait.
I savour every minute, cherish every hour
That we have spent together; there has been so much to share.

Then through the sunshine came a day, so horrible and grey
When I had to face the fact my Dad had gone away.
It's a fearful prospect that he'll be seen no more.
Death is so dreadful, that closing of the door
Never to be opened, there isn't any key.
I am on the outside, dear God, can he see me?

This grief is so awful, the pain I cannot bear.
No one there to comfort me, no one there to care.
Part of me died, when we laid my Dad to rest, but
I must carry on alone and try to do my best
To live with all my memories, and pray the pain will lessen
And be confident that one day, we will meet again in Heaven.

Christine Cuss

Notes

22 January 1935
This is a beautiful painting, Madonna of the Bay, painted by Agnes Tatham. I have three letters from the artist to my mother, one in which she says that she will pay my mother *2s 6d* for me to pose.

1 September 1935
We lived in the top flat of my grandparents' house in Hammersmith, London. They had a second home at Herne Bay, Kent, so we frequently went there for holidays.

30 January 1936
My grandfather, a former policeman, suffered from glaucoma and sadly went blind. As a little girl I used to walk with him with his white stick to the shop at the end of the road where he would buy his tobacco and some sweets for me. I loved him dearly.

16 August 1936
We were a very happy family, and enjoyed many days out.

31 December 1936
My parents attended the 'Old Year Out and the New Year In' services every year at the local Anglican Church.

January 1937
Faggy was my favourite rag doll – I took it everywhere.

24 March 1937
The boat race was a big event. Of course, there were no televisions in those days, so we went along the towpath by the River Thames and Hammersmith Bridge to watch it live.

16 June 1937
Uncle Tom was my mother's eldest brother, also a policeman. I loved the Ascot races, even more so in later life when I was able to watch from the Royal Enclosure.

2 August 1937
The past entries show how much we enjoyed outings as a family which also involved uncles and aunts. Dorothy was my uncle's wife.

21 August 1937
Uncle Percy was my father's brother who lived in Sheffield with his wife Lizzie.

15 September 1937
Cyril was Uncle Percy's son.

14 March 1938
Up until now my father's diary was a simple record of a very ordinary family who enjoyed days out, holidays

together and being members of a close family. I do not think my father intended it to be anything else, but from now it becomes much more serious, more than he could ever have envisaged.

16 July 1938
My parents threw me a birthday party each year. They could never have imagined that in a few years' time there would be a party with a big difference!

12 September 1938
Again, another worrying entry with the threat of war.

29 September 1938
The fear of war increases, so much so that my mother is anxious that she will be parted from me. A fear for many parents throughout the country.

13 November 1938
Joanie was my cousin, daughter of my father's brother Harold.

4 December 1938
Barbara was my cousin, daughter of my father's sister Eileen.

31 December 1938
My mother was a wonderful machinist who worked from home making blouses for a firm who supplied the

top shops in the West End of London. She often worked well into the night, leaving my father to cope with amusing me and doing household chores. They worked very much as a team.

22 July 1939
I remember this boil very well, particularly when my father gave me a piggy back and his folded arms behind his back supporting me bumped against the boil! I cried.

6 August 1939
My father's brother and his son.

13 August 1939
I regret that I cannot remember Beryl.

29 August 1939
So many families were trying to decide what to do and where to go to be safe. My parents thought that Eastbourne might be an option for my mother and I, away from London, then they tried staying with my father's brother, his wife and daughter in Hanworth for safety.

8 September 1939
The separation was too much.

30 November 1939
My parents must have been feeling so unhappy and desperate to know what to do for the best.

1 December 1939
I find this entry the most difficult to read. I can't bear to imagine what turmoil they must have gone through before coming to this decision, and the risks that could possibly be involved. They loved me so much. This was the day before I was due to be evacuated. Parents that had to face sending their children for evacuation to complete strangers must have been in total agony.

20 February 1940
Cartoon not found.

10 May 1940
Germany invaded Holland and Belgium. The story of what happened to one family in Belgium at this time has been recorded by me elsewhere. The two Belgian refugee brothers were 'adopted' by a family in Chiswick only a couple of miles away from where I was living.

N.B. Many years later I married into this family and through our friendship, which had then spanned fifty more years, my father's eldest brother's name was discovered on the Menin Gate in Ypres, a monument to all those young men who were lost without trace.

9 October 1940
At this time we used to seek refuge in an Anderson shelter built in our back garden. This was literally a large, deep hole in the ground which had a re-enforced curved

roof. When the siren rang in the night, we left our beds and huddled together with my grandparents in the shelter. It was cold and very miserable.

7 November 1940
Another tear-jerking entry for me to read. Yet another attempt to keep my mother and me safe away from the terrible bombing being experienced.

11 December 1940
In addition to all the horrors of war, people still had to cope with the stresses of bereavement in their families.

31 December 1940
The depth of winter and so much to cope with. It was bitterly cold in the shelter at night.

11 January 1941
My parents' anxieties were deepening.

12 March 1941
A great relief for my father not to be called up. As a young man he had a very bad accident with a knife and cut his eye. An operation was performed at St George's Hospital at Hyde Park which saved the sight in that eye. Throughout his life, whenever my father's eyes were examined, there was great interest in that eye by opticians and eye specialists.

27 March 1941

We, along with most of our neighbours, had transferred to a public air-raid shelter in our road where we went every night from 7 p.m. until around 7 a.m. There were two, one on each side of the road. There were bunks down each side, three tiers high and bench seats down the middle. There were no radios, of course, but sometimes someone would play a mouth organ and people would sing. People were very kind to each other in those days, offering support to each other, particularly if a telegram had been received notifying bad news from the front.

23 June 1941

It was not possible to have trips to the seaside anymore but we still kept our spirits up by having day trips to local places of interest.

29 July 1941

This must have been a nice break for my mother and me, which I believe was arranged by the local church.

31 December l941

Uncle Alf was my mother's younger brother, a 'red devil' Sixth Airborne Glider Division.

19 March 1942

Uncle Harold was my father's brother. Harold had a twin brother called Geoff.

11 August 1942
We were very into sports and athletics as Geoff was a fine athlete. My father was also very keen on ballroom dancing and taught me to dance at a very young age. Around the age of 16 I danced as an amateur and entered examinations for medals and competitions.

27 November 1942
Sadly, the little baby died.

20 January 1943
Years later I discovered that this was the first assignment my brother-in-law, John Whelan, had to cover as a young reporter working for the *Daily Express*.

4 March 1943
It was discovered that my mother was suffering from tinnitus.

28 July 1943
I was very sad at the death of my grandfather. I was told that he was with the angels.

9 August 1943
My grandmother had a second home at Herne Bay and this is the reason that we had visited so often in the past. On this occasion there were papers she needed following the death of my grandfather which were filed at her second home.

13 January 1944
The clothing book shows my National Registration (identity card) Number. My father made me memorise this number because he said that it was important. I can still remember it to this day.

20 February 1944
I am touched by my father's compassion for the German people.

23 February 1944
I remember this very clearly. Great Aunt Ada's daughter was trapped, lying under the heavy Victorian table, with her dead mother and husband beside her. She was unharmed but firemen were using hosepipes to stop a fire. She had been screaming but water was rising over her body until it almost reached her mouth. She knew that she had just one last scream. This was heard by a fireman and they started removing the rubble until they found her. She did not have a mark on her but just before lifting her out of the debris a brick fell on her forehead leaving a very bad injury. My grandmother nursed her for several weeks in her home in Hammersmith (the same house my parents shared with her).

6 April 1944
Uncle Geoff was my father's brother and twin to Harold.

23 June 1944

This is a day that can never be erased from my memory. Looking back, I could have been orphaned that night as both my parents had run back to our house, leaving me with my grandmother in the air-raid shelter. My father wanted to go to the toilet and my mother said that she would make a cup of tea. My mother heard a doodlebug coming, called to my father, and ran back to the shelter. Dad ran, but when he heard the noise of the craft stop, he threw himself on to the ground covering his head. There was a huge explosion. I awoke to find the air-raid shelter full of dust, people were screaming and crying, and I will never forget the look on my mother's face. Then an air-raid warden came into the shelter followed by my father. We walked the streets homeless with nothing but our lives and a small leather case which my father took to the air-raid shelter each night containing marriage certificates, bank books and important documents, including my baptismal certificate and his diary to me. We took refuge in a nearby shelter.

27 November 1944

Following the bombing, we lived with another family member. The local council told my parents that if they knew of anywhere that was empty, they would requisition the property and allow us to live there. This was done and we lived in the top flat of a Wimpey property. Another family had the two lower floors. My parents had to purchase utility furniture with dockets and were given blankets etc. which had been sent from Canada or Australia, I believe. It was very cold in the winter so we put our coats on top of the beds. The purchase of the piano shows how hard my parents were trying to make a home again.

12 December 1944
Many of my lessons at school were spent in air-raid shelters, as well as many of my evenings. I therefore learned to knit under supervision from adults and was rather good at it. I learned to knit socks for soldiers and became adept at turning heels. We did our best to support the troops, hence the letter from the stranger, Cedric Grant (see pp. 108–9).

14 February 1945
My mother worked as a dinner lady at the school I attended following the bombing, the school having been destroyed at the same time as our home. In passing, she remarked to one of the staff about the huge explosion the previous night. She then learned that it was in the area where her brother and family lived. Shocked, she left immediately to check if the family were okay, but when she arrived it was an area of devastation. She asked some children if they knew where the Morris family were, only to be told that they had all been killed. One of the other children rebuked the child for telling her and then directed her to a police information area. Yes, the whole family had gone. One of my cousins suffered

from polio and I believe only his leg in a calliper was found. Our family had suffered enough, particularly my grandmother. The tragedies we had experienced in the previous year were too much to bear.

24 February 1945
I believe my cousin Joan was one of the first GI brides to go to America and one of the first to come back!

8 May 1945
It is true, I have never forgotten the singing and dancing in the streets.

21 June 1945
A wonderful tribute from an American soldier.

11 July 1945
My father was determined that I should have the education that he never had. I make no apologies for the many spelling mistakes he made recording his diary. My parents had realised their ambition, and that was to give me the very best education. I had passed my entrance examination to the Godolphin and Latymer School, and I was on the threshold of great things to come. I feel very privileged and proud to be an 'Old Dolphin'. The school gave me not only a first-class education, but broadened my horizons and encouraged me to be a confident young woman.

It has been an emotional experience reading my father's diary again. I would like to pay tribute to my wonderful mother and father, particularly to my father for recording our experiences as a family throughout the Second World War. There were five pages left at the end of the book upon which no entries were written. This puzzled me, but I have been told that my father took me up to my memory. Yes, we had many, many happy memories after the war.